SNAPSHOTS IN HISTORY

THE TET OFFENSIVE

Turning Point of the Vietnam War

by Dale Anderson

THE TET OFFENSIVE

Turning Point of the Vietnam War

by Dale Anderson

Content Adviser: Derek Shouba, Adjunct History Professor
and Assistant Provost, Roosevelt University

Reading Adviser: Susan Kesselring, M.A., Literacy Educator,
Rosemount–Apple Valley–Eagan (Minnesota) School District

COMPASS POINT BOOKS

MINNEAPOLIS, MINNESOTA

COMPASS POINT BOOKS

3109 West 50th Street, #115
Minneapolis, MN 55410

Visit Compass Point Books on the Internet at
www.compasspointbooks.com
or e-mail your request to
custserv@compasspointbooks.com

For Compass Point Books
Jennifer VanVoorst, Jaime Martens, XNR Productions, Inc.,
Catherine Neitge, Keith Griffin, and Carol Jones

Produced by White-Thomson Publishing Ltd.
Tel.: 0044 (0)1273 403990
210 High Street, Lewes BN7 2NH

For White-Thomson Publishing
Stephen White-Thomson, Brian Krumm, Amy Sparks, Tinstar Design
Ltd. *www.tinstar.co.uk*, Derek Shouba, Joselito F. Seldera, Bill Hurd,
and Timothy Griffin

Library of Congress Cataloging-in-Publication Data
Anderson, Dale, 1953-
  The Tet Offensive : turning point of the Vietnam War / by Dale
Anderson.
      p. cm. — (Snapshots in history)
  Includes bibliographical references and index.
  ISBN 0-7565-1623-4 (hardcover)
  1. Tet Offensive, 1968—Juvenile literature. I. Title. II. Series.
  DS557.8.T4A53 2005
  959.704'34—dc22   2005027149

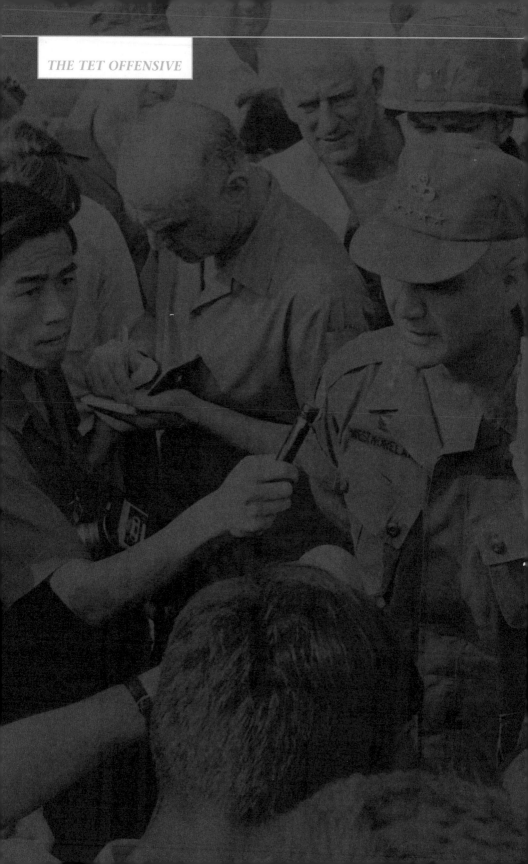

CONTENTS

Attack on the Embassy

Just after midnight on January 31, 1968, a small force of 19 Viet Cong fighters gathered in a dark building in Saigon, the capital of South Vietnam. Celebrations of Tet, the Vietnamese New Year, were under way in Vietnam, but the fighters had no plans to attend any festivities. Instead, they were quietly unpacking weapons and explosives. It was then that the rebels, led by two officers, learned what their mission was: to attack the U.S. Embassy in Saigon.

The Viet Cong were communist rebels fighting the government of South Vietnam. The United States was a major ally of South Vietnam. About 500,000 U.S. troops were stationed throughout the country to fight the Viet Cong and their allies from the North.

The Viet Cong fighters piled into a truck and a taxicab and drove to their target. Just before 3 A.M., as they drove past the night gate, the Viet Cong opened fire on the two American guards stationed there. The military police officers (MPs) returned fire and then ducked inside the 8-foot (2.4-meter) wall that surrounded the embassy grounds. They closed and locked the steel gate and quickly sent out an alert that the embassy was being attacked.

The U.S. Embassy's night gate was along the street on one side of the building. Thong Nhut Boulevard ran along the front. The Viet Cong attackers blew a hole in a section of the wall surrounding the embassy.

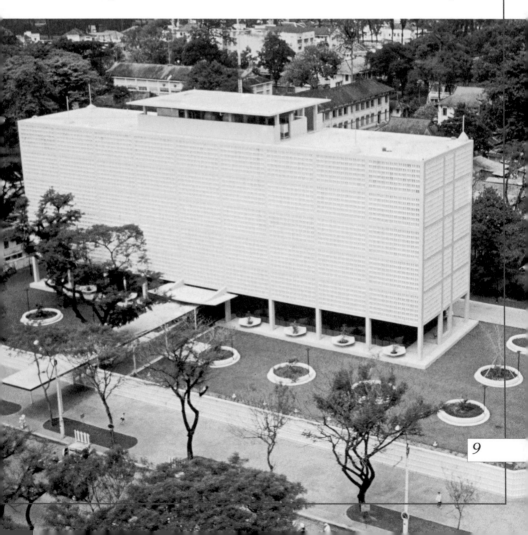

The truck and cab turned right onto Thong Nhut Boulevard, the wide street in front of the embassy. A sapper—an explosives expert—jumped out of his vehicle. He placed a stack of explosives at the base of one section of the wall. When he set off the charge, it blew a 3-foot (1-m) hole in the wall.

The two Viet Cong officers charged through the hole. With a direct line of fire, the American MPs shot them dead. One MP shouted into his radio:

They're coming in! They're coming in!

Seconds later, the MP and his partner were killed by other Viet Cong soldiers who had crawled through the hole.

Two U.S. MPs patrolling the city had heard the guards' initial alert. Their jeep sped down Thong Nhut Boulevard toward the enemy vehicles. However, Viet Cong fighters waiting outside the wall cut them down in a barrage of gunfire. Within minutes, the remaining Viet Cong fighters stood inside the wall on the embassy grounds.

A SAPPER'S TRAINING

Sappers went through rigorous training. Nguyen Van Mo, a sapper in North Vietnam's army, recalled that they had to learn "how to crouch while walking, how to crawl, how to move silently through mud and water, how to walk through dry leaves." They had to move slowly and carefully to avoid being seen by lookouts or searchlights. They also had to learn patience:

Time made no difference. In training it might take two or three hours to crawl through five fences of barbed wire.

The U.S. Embassy was now protected by only three guards: two in the lobby and one on the roof. Six more Americans worked inside the building that night, but they had only small hand weapons. Two more Americans were in a house behind the embassy—with only one grenade to defend themselves. The Americans were outnumbered and outarmed. They knew they would have to act quickly.

A U.S. soldier stood near the bodies of two MPs who were killed during the attack on the U.S. Embassy.

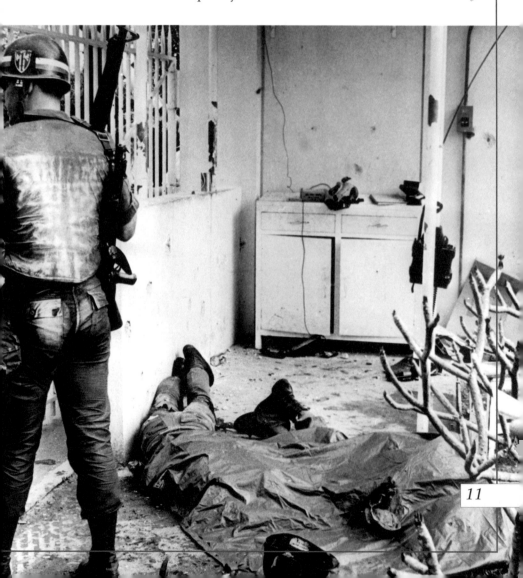

In the lobby, U.S. Marine Sergeant Ronald Harper slammed shut the embassy's heavy wooden door and locked it. As he ran down the hall to get more weapons, bullets ripped into the lobby. A rocket smashed through the outer wall, showering debris inside the main entrance, and knocked out the only two radios in the lobby. Corporal George Zahuranic, the other guard in the lobby, was wounded in the attack.

As more rockets slammed into the building, Harper returned to give first aid to Zahuranic. He was certain the attackers would force their way into the building, but the Viet Cong never entered. Their officers were dead, and they had no clear orders of how to proceed. They stayed on the embassy grounds and continued to fire at the building, but they never tried to blow the door open.

On the roof, Sergeant Rudy Soto, the only other American guard, could do nothing to help Harper and Zahuranic. His shotgun had jammed when he tried to fire. All he could do was empty the six shots in his revolver and watch the attackers.

Reinforcements arrived quickly. Marine Captain Robert O'Brien gathered a force of MPs at a nearby barracks and raced several blocks to the embassy. The locked night gate prevented them from entering, as did gunfire from the Viet Cong inside.

Meanwhile, word of the attack spread. Phone calls carried the news to several reporters. One,

who worked for the Associated Press, a news agency, sent a quick report back to his headquarters in the United States. That report was filed just half an hour after the attack began.

More U.S. forces gathered on the streets outside, but they felt no need for urgency. As one soldier explained:

> The [Viet Cong] are inside the compound, they're not going anyplace. Nobody can get in, nobody can get out. [The commander] says try to wait here until daylight 'cause we got 'em inside.

Viet Cong gunfire initially prevented helicopters from landing on the embassy roof. However, they could be landed on the street outside the embassy grounds for soldiers to deliver ammunition, and blood for wounded soldiers.

13

The officer in charge wanted armored cars and helicopters before attacking, but bringing them in would take time. While they waited, U.S. soldiers on the street and on top of nearby buildings shot at anything they saw move on the embassy grounds.

Once they got inside the embassy walls, U.S. soldiers moved quickly to secure the area.

At five in the morning, a helicopter attempted to land on the flat embassy roof. Heavy gunfire from the Viet Cong on the ground forced the pilot to leave. An hour later, another chopper did land. It dropped off ammunition for M-16 rifles and then left with the wounded Zahuranic. The ammunition would do no good, however. None of the Americans inside the embassy had M-16s.

At dawn, U.S. soldiers blew open the lock on the front gate and entered the grounds. A jeep plowed through the broken gate, with soldiers streaming in behind. They quickly spotted most of the remaining Viet Cong fighters and shot them.

One Viet Cong fighter ran into a house behind the embassy. U.S. troops fired tear gas into the house to drive him out. Diplomat George Jacobson, who lived inside the house, raced to a window on the second floor and frantically shouted down for a weapon. He figured the soldier would move up to the second floor to avoid the gas.

The Americans threw Jacobson a pistol and a gas mask. He grabbed them and ducked back inside to hide in a corner. Soon after, the Viet Cong fighter rushed into the room, spraying bullets from his gun. Jacobson felled him with one shot. The battle for the embassy was over.

Meanwhile, another helicopter had been able to land on the embassy roof. Soldiers piled out and entered the building from above. They did a slow and careful room-to-room search of the embassy, but they found no Viet Cong fighters.

15

The Viet Cong struck other targets in Saigon at the same time they hit the embassy. Military police captured this man in one of the other fights.

16

Shortly after 9 A.M., the embassy was officially declared clear of all enemy fighters. General William Westmoreland, commander of all U.S. forces in Vietnam, strode onto the embassy grounds in a clean, pressed uniform. Westmoreland told reporters that the attack on the embassy had been part of a wider Viet Cong assault across Vietnam.

He complained that the Viet Cong had broken a holiday truce to stage these attacks. The attacks are called the Tet Offensive because they occurred during the Tet holiday.

Westmoreland tried to reassure the reporters that things were under control. He told them:

TET

Tet is the Vietnamese New Year, but the holiday is far more important to the Vietnamese people than New Year celebrations are to people in the United States. Tet is a time to celebrate family and honor one's ancestors. People celebrate the holiday for a week, although the first three days are the most special. Shots and shell explosions that rang out on the night of the Tet Offensive in 1968 were mistaken for holiday fireworks by some.

The enemy's well-laid plans went afoul. Some superficial damage was done to the building. All of the enemy that entered the compound so far as I can determine were killed. Nineteen bodies have been found on the premises—enemy bodies.

However, as Americans moved back into the embassy building, they passed a troubling sight. To one side of the door, the seal of the United States had once stood on a heavy piece of granite. That seal had tumbled to the ground, knocked down by a Viet Cong rocket. As the next days and weeks unfolded, the U.S. effort in Vietnam would be badly shaken as well. ◤

The War in Vietnam

The Tet Offensive was a turning point in the struggle for control of Vietnam, but the roots of the conflict stretched deep into Vietnam's past. In the late 1800s, France seized Vietnam and neighboring countries as colonies. It held these lands for many decades. Some Vietnamese, however, yearned for independence. One of them was Ho Chi Minh. In the 1920s, he became a communist and began working for the independence of Vietnam.

After France was conquered by Germany in World War II, Germany's ally Japan seized France's colonies in Southeast Asia. Ho Chi Minh formed a group called the Viet Minh to fight for the independence of Vietnam. In August 1945, Japan was defeated in World War II. The Viet Minh quickly took control of Hanoi, which was then the capital of Vietnam.

Ho Chi Minh led his followers against France in the 1940s and 1950s and against the United States in the 1960s and 1970s.

On September 2, 1945, before a large crowd, Ho proclaimed the independence of Vietnam. Echoing the U.S. Declaration of Independence, he said:

> *We hold the truth that all men are created equal, that they are endowed by their Creator with certain unalienable rights, among them life, liberty, and the pursuit of happiness.*

France, however, did not see Vietnam as independent and wanted to regain control of its colonies. It sent an army to the southern part of Vietnam, which Ho's forces did not control. A bitter war broke out between France and the Viet Minh, which lasted from 1946 until 1954. In 1954, Ho's forces surrounded a large French army near the northern city of Dien Bien Phu. The French soldiers were outnumbered nearly four to one. Vietnamese artillery battered them while Viet Minh soldiers dug trenches that inched closer to the French lines. After many weeks, the French general surrendered more than 10,000 men.

HO CHI MINH (1890–1969)

Ho Chi Minh was born in Nguyen Tat Thanh, a village in northern Vietnam. He spent many years in Europe, where he became a communist. In 1919, he asked world leaders to end French control of Vietnam. The request was never considered, but it made him famous in his own country. He returned to Vietnam in 1941, taking the name Ho Chi Minh, which means "he who enlightens."

The Vietnamese victory was decisive—and timely. The very next day, peace talks began

in Geneva, Switzerland. Tired of the bloody war and disheartened by the defeat at Dien Bien Phu, the French were ready to grant Vietnam its independence.

However, the United States would not accept a communist government in Vietnam. After long and difficult talks, the parties involved made an agreement. Vietnam would be temporarily divided into two sections. Ho would govern in the North. In the South, Bo Dai—the traditional emperor of Vietnam—would rule. Elections would be held in two years. At that point, if the Vietnamese people wanted, their country could be united under one government.

France sent more troops to Dien Bien Phu by parachute during the siege of the city, but in the end, the French forces surrendered to the Vietnamese who surrounded them.

21

However, the planned elections never took place. The United States and leaders in the South feared that Ho's supporters would win the election, and so they refused to allow the vote. As a result, Vietnam stayed a divided country. Ho led the communist North Vietnam. The United States

Vietnamese Emperor Bo Dai (left) met with French President Vincent Auriol during discussions about Vietnam's future.

supported the anticommunist South Vietnam. Ngo Dinh Diem became South Vietnam's first president in 1955, after he ousted Bo Dai.

These events angered many people who wanted to form a communist state of their own in South Vietnam. As a result, rebels in the South formed a group called the National Liberation Front (NLF). The NLF was referred to as the Viet Cong by the South Vietnamese government and people. "Viet Cong" was an insulting slang term for "Vietnamese Communist." The Viet Cong soon began to fight to overthrow South Vietnam's leaders.

North Vietnam gave supplies to the Viet Cong. Many of the supplies flowed down a path worn into the dense rain forests of Laos and Cambodia, to the west of Vietnam. That path was called the Ho Chi Minh Trail. Sometimes soldiers from the People's Army of North Vietnam (PAVN) provided supplies as well.

The United States viewed the Viet Cong with alarm. American leaders feared that if South Vietnam fell to communism, nearby countries would, too. They believed that a change to communist rule could never be undone. For these reasons, the U.S. government began sending money, weapons, and military advisers to South Vietnam.

But the situation in South Vietnam grew worse. Ngo Dinh Diem was accused of corruption after members of his family became rich by pocketing some of the American aid or by selling positions in the government or the army.

In November 1963, South Vietnamese military officers killed Ngo Dinh Diem and his brother and then took control of the government. U.S. officials who had been tipped off in advance had told the officers that they would not oppose the move.

That same month, Lyndon Johnson became president of the United States after President John F. Kennedy was assassinated. Johnson faced a difficult decision about what to do in Vietnam. Johnson was not sure the United States could win a war in Vietnam, and he worried that if he used American force too quickly, he would draw communist China or the Soviet Union into the war. That, he feared, could start World War III.

On the other hand, Johnson also believed that doing nothing would hurt the United States. If the Viet Cong won the war, he thought, the United States would look weak, and Southeast Asia would become a communist region. Unsure of what action to take, Johnson sent more advisers and financial aid to South Vietnam. Then in August 1964, word reached Washington, D.C., that a U.S. Navy ship had been attacked by North Vietnamese ships in the Gulf of Tonkin, off the coast of North Vietnam.

A few days later, the U.S. Congress approved a resolution that gave the president authority to "take all necessary measures" to defend U.S. forces and prevent further attacks. The resolution gave Johnson the power to take whatever action he thought best in Vietnam, with support from the American people.

Johnson did not take any action right away. In late 1964, Viet Cong fighters attacked U.S. forces in Saigon on two occasions. Both times aides urged Johnson to bomb North Vietnam. Both times Johnson chose to do nothing.

Lyndon Johnson was sworn in as president after his predecessor, John F. Kennedy, was assassinated in Dallas, Texas.

25

President Johnson sent thousands of U.S. soldiers to fight in South Vietnam. Helicopters gave U.S. ground troops in Vietnam great mobility.

Early in 1965, the president changed his mind. By this time, several of his aides were telling him that the government of South Vietnam could never become stable in the face of Viet Cong attacks. The Viet Cong, they said, would continue the attacks as long as the United States did nothing.

Then, in February 1965, the Viet Cong twice attacked a U.S. military base at Pleiku, in central South Vietnam. These attacks convinced Johnson that a strong reaction was necessary, and he ordered air strikes against targets in North Vietnam. By early March, air raids were taking place every day in a massive bombing campaign called Operation Rolling Thunder. By 1967, U.S. planes had dropped more tons of bombs on North Vietnam than they had on Germany and Japan combined during World War II.

President Johnson also sent more U.S. ground troops to South Vietnam. By July 1965, there were 75,000 U.S. soldiers in Vietnam.

By December 1965, there were about 200,000 troops. A year later, the number had skyrocketed to nearly 500,000.

These troops faced a difficult task. The Viet Cong fought a guerrilla war. They staged attacks with mortars and machine guns against U.S. bases, but after a quick fight, they slipped away into trees and bushes, only to reappear later and attack again. When U.S. soldiers moved into the jungle to find them, the Viet Cong simply crept away.

The growing combat effort meant that the number of U.S. casualties began to mount. People in the United States began to protest against the war. They were angry about growing American casualties—and by the rising number of Vietnamese civilians killed or wounded by the war. They also protested against the draft, the system used to bring young American men into the army. Tens of thousands of people joined protest marches.

THE DRAFT

During the Vietnam War, when men turned 18 they had to register for the draft. Local draft boards decided who would be sent into the army. Some men were excused for physical or religious reasons, or because they were college students. Critics charged that wealthier people were able to avoid the draft more easily than the poor. They also pointed out that African-Americans made up a disproportionately large share of the army. In 1973, the United States ended the draft and adopted an all-volunteer army.

By late 1967, the war had grown costly in terms of both money and lives. And it had begun to deeply divide the American people. ◣

Buildup to Tet

By 1967, the war was becoming a nightmare for the Viet Cong and the North Vietnamese too. The U.S. bombing campaign hit North Vietnam hard. The bombs killed and wounded many people. In addition, some of North Vietnam's political and military leaders worried that the destruction would hurt their country's efforts to build industry. Some feared that the bombing was a preparation for a U.S. invasion of the North.

In April 1967, North Vietnam's Politburo debated what to do. This group of 11 government officials made the major decisions for the government of North Vietnam. General Vo Nguyen Giap, commander of the North Vietnamese army, was a member of the Politburo. He had launched two major attacks on U.S. troops in 1965. His troops had suffered

heavy losses, convincing him that he could not beat the Americans in open battle. General Giap urged leaving the fighting to the South Vietnamese Viet Cong and using a long guerrilla war to wear down American willingness to fight.

In 1967, top leaders in North Vietnam debated how to answer heavy U.S. bombing in North Vietnam.

However, other members of the Politburo argued that the Viet Cong could not bring about a communist revolution in the South alone. They thought that the North should launch an attack to turn the tide of the war.

In July 1967, the Politburo members came to an agreement:

> *[The South should stage a] spontaneous uprising ... in order to win a decisive victory in a short time."*

At the same time, there would be a general offensive in the South that would include Viet Cong and North Vietnamese troops. The members

of the Politburo thought that this military uprising combined with a general uprising would convince the Americans to stop bombing the North and begin peace talks.

Leaders of the National Liberation Front agreed to the plan. They often worried that North Vietnam and the United States might ignore them when peace talks finally began and hoped that by taking part in an important victory, they would gain a say in any peace settlement.

General Giap drew up a three-part plan for the offensive. First, he would launch a major attack of North Vietnamese forces against U.S. troops in the northern part of South Vietnam. He hoped that this would draw more U.S. troops to that area, weakening their hold on cities in South Vietnam.

The second part of the plan was to attack as many cities as possible. Giap hoped that the attacks would show people that the cities were not safe, weakening their faith in the Americans and breaking down their support for the government of South Vietnam.

The third part of the plan was to use political efforts to try to bring about a general uprising in the South. At best, this revolt could topple the South Vietnamese government. At worst, it would at least shake American confidence in that government.

General Vo Nguyen Giap, the victor over French troops at Dien Bien Phu, was in charge of North Vietnam's defenses.

31

Over the course of 1967, the North and the Viet Cong prepared for the offensive, which was to take place that winter and the following spring. Troops, weapons, and supplies were moved south. Almost 100 tons (90 metric tons) of weapons and supplies were hauled to the Saigon area alone.

Troops also learned more about their selected targets. Lieutenant Tuan Van Ban of the North Vietnamese army later remembered how he and his fellow soldiers studied one target:

PREPARING FOR THE ATTACK

Preparing for the Tet Offensive took months. Equipment had to be trucked down the long Ho Chi Minh Trail from the North to the South. The Viet Cong used oxcarts, bicycles, and small boats to do this work, and those vehicles could only carry small amounts at a time. Some methods were very clever. Large, heavy weapons were carried into Saigon inside fake coffins.

> *Weeks before, as part of a small [scouting] team, we had crawled and cut our way through the mines and barbed wire to get a close look at the base. We drew maps of the layout, including the positions of all the bunkers and buildings so our mortar men could preplan their targets.*

Other preparations were needed as well. Forgers made false identification papers to allow some Viet Cong to move into the cities to help plan and carry out the attacks. Political leaders made plans to take over city governments if the attacks managed to topple them.

Eventually, General Giap settled on the Vietnamese holiday of Tet as the occasion for the attack. He expected that, as in earlier years, both sides would agree on a truce for the holiday. As a result, the Americans and the South Vietnamese army would be less alert.

As they moved supplies from North Vietnam to South Vietnam, soldiers had to deal with dense rain forest and fast-running rivers, as well as U.S. bombing attacks.

But Tet also had symbolic importance in the history of Vietnam. In 1789, Quang Trung, then emperor of Vietnam, led his forces into Hanoi during Tet to overthrow an occupying army sent from China. His victory was a proud moment in Vietnam's history—one that the Viet Cong and the North Vietnamese hoped to duplicate.

The Americans and the South Vietnamese saw clues that something big was coming. Intelligence reports indicated that there was heavier traffic along the Ho Chi Minh Trail than usual. One captured document revealed that attacks would hit "cities and towns, base areas, airfields, and lines of communication." Another contained information about the goal of demoralizing South Vietnamese troops. Finally, several documents showed that the communists hoped attacks on cities would cause a general uprising.

But the captured documents did not reveal exactly when the attacks would take place. Also, none of them made it clear that Saigon would be a target, too.

While the communists made their preparations, the U.S. government was trying to raise morale at home. By the summer of 1967, however, several U.S. newspapers that had previously supported the war began to express doubts about it. By October, a public opinion poll showed that, for the first time, more people thought the war was a mistake than supported it. Around that time, tens of thousands of people marched in peace rallies in cities across the country. One march of many thousands led to the doors of the Pentagon—the headquarters of the United States Defense Department.

President Johnson wanted to shore up support for the war. He brought General William Westmoreland, who was commanding the U.S. forces, back to Washington, D.C., to tell Congress and the American people about progress in the war.

Westmoreland cited statistics on the number of enemy fighters killed in recent months and the number of villages no longer under Viet Cong control. In one speech, he told listeners:

With 1968 [approaching], a new phase is now starting. We have reached an important point when the end begins to come into view ... [Our plans for the future show] some light at the end of the tunnel.

A large crowd gathered outside the Pentagon in Washington, D.C., on October 21, 1967, to protest U.S. involvement in the Vietnam War.

35

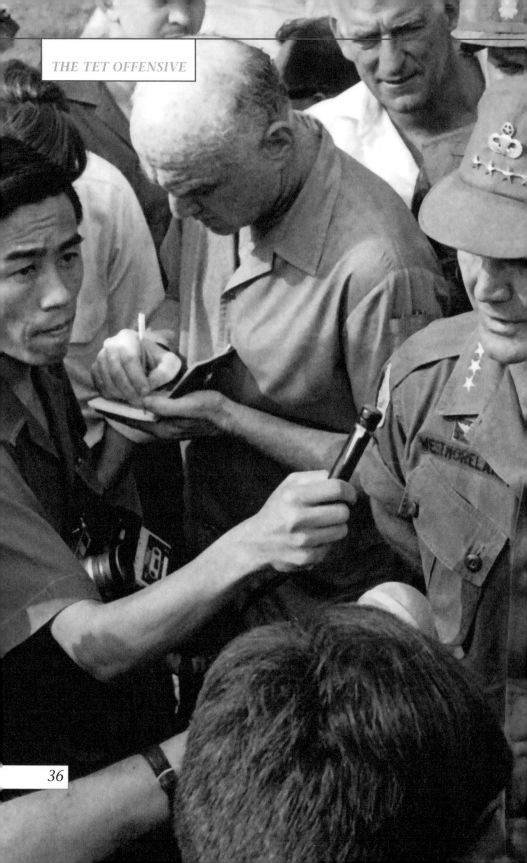

Westmoreland even said that he could foresee a time when American troops could start to leave South Vietnam. The message from the government was clear: The war was going well.

Meanwhile, fighting in Vietnam had taken a new turn. In late October, the Viet Cong attacked and seized the town of Loc Ninh, north of Saigon. The fighters used unusual tactics for the Viet Cong. They attacked in force and kept up the attacks for several days despite being subjected to heavy artillery shelling and bombing. In the past, Viet Cong troops had pulled back when met with such firepower.

On November 3, 1967, soldiers from the People's Army of North Vietnam (PAVN) launched an attack on a base at Dak To. This was an isolated spot in the northern highlands of South Vietnam. Once again, Americans were surprised by the size of the enemy force and the duration of the attack, which lasted three weeks.

General William Westmoreland, commander of U.S. forces in South Vietnam, frequently talked to the press. A speech he made in Washington, D.C., late in 1967, suggested that the war situation was improving.

After Westmoreland returned to Vietnam, the communists staged an even larger attack. This one targeted a small U.S. Marine base at Khe Sanh, near the border between North and South Vietnam. An estimated 22,000 PAVN troops faced just over 6,000 Marines. More U.S. troops were pulled out of cities and sent to posts near Khe Sanh in case they would be needed to help the Marines.

Fierce fighting started on January 21, 1968, and continued for weeks. Each day, the PAVN troops dropped mortars on the Marines' positions. By night, U.S. bombers dumped thousands of tons

U.S. Marines stood atop their tanks in Khe Sanh as bombs dropped from planes battered PAVN soldiers attacking the northern base.

of bombs on the PAVN troops who surrounded Khe Sanh. Westmoreland was determined to hold the base. He told his staff:

> *We are not, repeat* not, *going to be defeated at Khe Sanh. I will tolerate no talking or even thinking to the contrary.*

At the end of January, Westmoreland and his troops would have to deal with greater problems than Khe Sanh. They would be facing attacks all over South Vietnam.

The Early Attacks

Chapter

4

The two sides had agreed to stop fighting and hold a truce during the Tet holiday that began on January 30, 1968. However, intelligence reports and recent attacks made U.S. officials uneasy. As a result, Nguyen Van Thieu, who was elected president of South Vietnam in 1967, cut the Tet truce for his troops to only 36 hours. But his order was not passed along to all his troops.

Meanwhile, General Westmoreland canceled the truce for his army and warned all troops to be on maximum alert. But the U.S. troops had heard so many such orders in the past and seen nothing happen that most of them ignored the warning.

Just before midnight on January 30, Hanoi's official government radio station broadcast a

special message. It was a poem written by Ho Chi Minh:

> *This spring far outshines the previous springs,*
> *Of victories throughout the land come happy tidings.*
> *Let South and North emulate each other in fighting the U.S. aggressors!*
> *Forward!*
> *Total victory shall be ours.*

The poem was a coded signal that the attacks should begin.

When communist troops finally launched the Tet Offensive on January 30 and 31, 1968, they hit many targets, and they hit hard. Attackers hit several locations in Saigon, one of them being the U.S. Embassy. Others struck at 36 of the 44 provincial capitals of South Vietnam and four other major cities. They also hit more than 70 district capitals and countless airfields and bases. It was a stunning display of coordinated attacks.

General John Chaisson of the U.S. Marines said:

> [The attacks were] surprisingly well-coordinated, surprisingly intensive, and launched with a surprising amount of [fearlessness].

Despite all the warnings, the attacks of the Tet Offensive came as a surprise.

The first attack was at Nha Trang, about halfway up South Vietnam's coast. Just past midnight on January 30, a South Vietnamese guard outside a radio station spotted soldiers getting out of two cars nearby. They wore uniforms of the Army of the Republic of South Vietnam (ARVN), but they acted strangely.

Suspicious, the guard fired at them, and they shot back. He alerted other guards, and they prevented the soldiers from capturing the radio station. Nha Trang was also hit by shelling from mortars and a ground attack by about 800 North Vietnamese troops. However, the South Vietnamese in the area easily beat back the attacks. The attack failed completely.

While the struggle went on at Nha Trang, other fights broke out. Over the next several hours, attackers hit Ban Me Thuot, Pleiku, and Kontum in the highlands and Da Nang and Qui Nhon on the coast.

At Ban Me Thuot, South Vietnamese troops were ready for an attack. They had captured plans for the assault, and Colonel Dao Quang An had taken forceful steps to defend the city. He sent patrols outside the city to intercept the attackers.

But a large Viet Cong force—about 2,000 troops—managed to fight its way into the city. They continued shooting, even though crowds of civilians were still celebrating the Tet holiday in the streets. The Viet Cong seized the provincial government building and the police station.

Explosions rocked a village as a U.S. ranger—a specially trained fighter— ran for cover. Viet Cong attackers hit several bases, cities, and villages of northern South Vietnam during the Tet Offensive.

Colonel An's ARVN troops soon responded with a counterattack. Using tanks and machine guns mounted on armored personnel carriers, they began firing back. Civilians scattered to escape the crossfire.

Troops who were defending positions in the city of Pleiku, located in central Vietnam, were also prepared for an attack. On January 5, 1968, U.S. soldiers had obtained a document detailing the

FALSE HOPES

Typically, the Viet Cong hit a target and slipped away before they could be captured. But in the Tet attacks, they were told to hold the captured positions with the promise that reinforcements would be sent. Those promises were false, though. Viet Cong leaders committed most of their combat strength to the offensive, leaving no reserves to use as reinforcements.

Viet Cong units that would be used in an attack and the targets they would strike. U.S. forces were ready when the attack came, and one high-ranking ARVN officer had placed several tanks in the city center.

As a result, the Viet Cong attackers were met with heavy firepower. The defense of the area might have gone even better if the ARVN commander had been more effective, but General Vinh Loc was not a forceful leader. He had been celebrating Tet in Saigon, and upon returning to the area, the general focused his attention on an effort to drive attacking troops away from his own home. However, all of the attacking forces were driven out of Pleiku after five days.

U.S. Marines used tanks and machine guns to counter attacks by Viet Cong fighters in northern South Vietnam.

45

The ARVN defenders at Kontum, located about 20 miles (32 km) north of Pleiku, faced a special challenge—some of the attacking units wore the uniforms of South Vietnam's regional defense forces. They hoped to use their disguises to sneak toward the home of a government official and several other key sites. However, the disguise was discovered, and real regional defense forces around the home struck back. Though that part of the attack was blocked, other Viet Cong units did occupy many parts of the city.

The battles of the Tet Offensive took place all over South Vietnam.

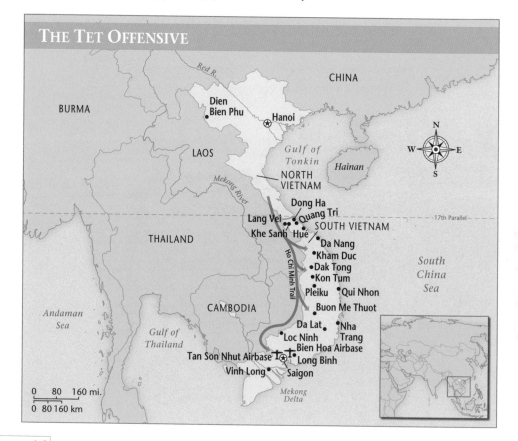

THE TET OFFENSIVE

The Viet Cong also attacked Da Nang, South Vietnam's second largest city, which was located on the coast of northern South Vietnam. Communist troops struck toward ARVN headquarters there, but the South Vietnamese commander responded forcefully. Though the enemy troops were only about 200 yards (182 m) from his headquarters, General Hoang Xuan Lam ordered air strikes against them. The heavy bombing silenced the attackers. Then the general ordered helicopter gunships to pursue the rest. The attack on Da Nang was ended quickly.

While Viet Cong infantry attacked at Qui Nhon, a city on the coast of central South Vietnam, a small group of fighters took control of the radio station. They carried messages that had been recorded earlier and described communist victories and ARVN surrenders across the country. Their purpose, of course, was to undermine support for the South Vietnamese government and to convince ARVN fighters to give up. They were unable to send out their message, however, because they were forced out of the station later in the day. ◣

The Main Attacks

As U.S. officers filed into their Saigon headquarters on the morning of January 31, 1968, they began receiving reports of the early attacks. General Phillip Davidson, the top intelligence officer, said to General Westmoreland:

> This is going to happen in the rest of the country tonight or tomorrow morning.

Westmoreland nodded in agreement.

The next night proved Davidson right, as many more attacks took place. Dozens of cities were hit early in the morning on January 31. Several points in and around Saigon itself were targeted. As at Qui Nhon the previous night, one target was a government radio station.

Viet Cong raiders had keys to get into the station, provided by someone who had worked there and copied the keys. However, a quick-thinking ARVN officer had warned those working at the station to take the station off the air if an attack took place, and a technician did so. Though the Viet Cong were able to take over the station, they could do nothing with it. Unable to broadcast, they destroyed all the equipment they found.

Armored personnel carriers rumbled down the streets of Saigon in the effort to clear the city of Viet Cong fighters.

Other attacks in Saigon hit the presidential palace and the headquarters of the South Vietnamese army and navy. None of these attacks gained their objectives, which included taking over the buildings, though at each site the attackers fought fiercely. Smaller attacks struck at barracks used by Americans. In all of the attacks, the Viet Cong hoped to induce large-scale surrenders, which would permit the installation of Viet Cong authority in the cities. At the very least, the Viet Cong aimed to undermine military and civilian confidence in the South Vietnamese government.

49

Tan Son Nhut Airbase, west of the city, and Bien Hoa Airbase, about 15 miles (24 km) north of the city, were two of the major targets near Saigon. These made up the hub of U.S. air operations. They were the two busiest airports in the world at the time.

Viet Cong forces attacked Tan Son Nhut Airbase from three directions, with the most serious threat coming from the west. Viet Cong fighters blew up one guard station and chased the guards from another. Soon they were streaming onto the airfield. U.S. soldiers formed a defensive line and held the Viet Cong off until morning. Also quick to respond were helicopters carrying rockets and machine guns, which were in the air and on the way to the airport within minutes of the attack. The helicopters met a hail of bullets, as Captain Chad Payne related:

> *I received fire everywhere I turned. My [helicopters] received seven hits, but this was nothing considering the amount of ground fire directed toward us. I've never seen anything like it.*

ATTACK AT BIEN HOA

Airports, headquarters buildings, and similar sites had rarely been the scene of combat before the Tet Offensive. Soldiers there faced the possibility of death for the first time. Stephen Howard served as an army photographer. He later recalled what it was like at Bien Hoa:

We went to war. Cooks, mechanics, detail men, everybody. And we had people in Bien Hoa that never shot a weapon out of basic training. And all through Tet there was this fear for them for the first time: I might get killed.

They came just in time: In one area of the airport, about 30 American soldiers faced more than 300 attackers. The helicopters fired rockets that blasted holes in the Viet Cong lines.

The Bien Hoa Airbase near Saigon was massive. U.S. fighter planes, ready for use in attacks or bombing raids, lined the field.

51

Later, armored units reached the scene and struck the Viet Cong from behind. The Viet Cong suffered badly. About 150 survivors withdrew to a nearby textile mill, where they were pounded by bombs.

Meanwhile, at Bien Hoa Airbase, Viet Cong mortars shelled defenses, and then infantry moved toward the air base. U.S. armored cavalry quickly moved to the area, though they faced obstacles. The Viet Cong had lined the roads approaching the base with snipers and other defenses.

However, the armored personnel carriers managed to reach the base and combined with other forces to drive the Viet Cong off. Still, the attackers blew up a building on the airbase and destroyed two fighter jets.

Near Bien Hoa Airbase was Long Binh, home to a huge ammunition depot. The Viet Cong sent a small force of sappers to attack the installation. They succeeded in planting enough charges to set off a massive explosion that destroyed more than $1.6 million worth of ammunition.

Fighting in Saigon and other cities left terrible destruction and some children without parents to take care of them.

By late on January 31, the major bases near Saigon had been secured. Viet Cong fighters had pulled back, however, into residential areas and any other place they could hide. It took several weeks before U.S. and ARVN troops could declare the city safe.

Fighting was still taking place in other parts of South Vietnam. At 2 A.M. on January 31, Viet Cong sappers set off explosions in Quang Tri, a provincial capital near the northern border of South Vietnam.

The People's Army of North Vietnam (PAVN) infantry attack was delayed by rain and rising water. As a result, they did not arrive until just over two hours later. They struck from the east, drove into the city, and held strong positions against a small ARVN force. The situation in Quang Tri remained very dangerous.

Viet Cong forces also attacked Da Lat. Both sides had an unspoken agreement not to bring combat to this beautiful mountain resort, located about 150 miles (240 km) northeast of Saigon. As a result, the city was lightly defended, making it an inviting target. Mortars and rockets destroyed a building that housed U.S. military police. The ARVN commander at Da Lat resourcefully

ARVN TROOPS

Several problems undermined the effectiveness of ARVN troops, the soldiers from South Vietnam. Many officers had gained command not because of their skill but through political connections. Troops also had outdated weapons and lacked radios and other important gear. Training was often poor as well. Still, many ARVN units performed effectively in the fighting at Tet, but only when their commanders showed skill and spirit.

put together a small force of South Vietnamese along with a few U.S. soldiers in the city to hold off the Viet Cong attack. The Viet Cong were able to secure the airfield, however, which blocked reinforcements and ammunition from reaching the city.

The Viet Cong also launched many attacks in the delta of the Mekong River, south of Saigon. American presence in the delta was minor, with about 1,600 military advisers attached to ARVN units, about as many combat troops, and a few airplanes, helicopters, and specially designed infantry transport boats.

U.S. soldiers had to respond quickly to the Tet attacks, as the Viet Cong hit many targets at the same time.

55

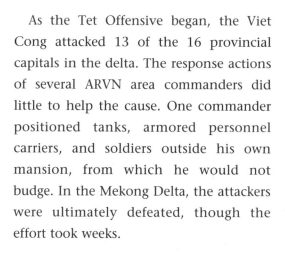

As the Tet Offensive began, the Viet Cong attacked 13 of the 16 provincial capitals in the delta. The response actions of several ARVN area commanders did little to help the cause. One commander positioned tanks, armored personnel carriers, and soldiers outside his own mansion, from which he would not budge. In the Mekong Delta, the attackers were ultimately defeated, though the effort took weeks.

Finally, the North Vietnamese hit the city of Hué. This city, the third largest in South Vietnam, was only about 50 miles (80 km) from the border of North Vietnam. Hué had once been the capital of Vietnam. The Perfume River divided the city into northern and southern parts. Dominating the north bank was a complex of buildings called the Citadel. Inside, along the narrow streets, stood the old imperial palace, temples, and other buildings, as well as homes and gardens. During the Vietnam War, an ARVN headquarters was located near the Citadel. Seven miles (11 km) of high defensive walls surrounded the Citadel. Treasured for its beauty by the Vietnamese, Hué had hardly been touched during the war. That communist troops would attack this city came as a great surprise.

Armored boats carried U.S. soldiers along the Mekong River in the delta region, which was south of Saigon.

Marines huddled for safety by a tank in the city of Hué.

At 3:40 in the morning on January 31, mortar shells and rockets slammed into the Citadel walls and other defensive spots. Two battalions of PAVN troops raced toward the Citadel from the west. Another battalion moved against targets in the southern part of Hué. Two more took positions across Highway 1—one north of the city and the other south of it. Their job was to block any enemy reinforcements coming from either direction.

PAVN troops rushed to take over the airport and the ARVN headquarters north of the Citadel. A crack unit of ARVN troops, the Black Panther Company, saved the airport and then joined other troops to beat back the attack on the headquarters. The PAVN backed off and moved into the Citadel. They took control of the old imperial palace and many other buildings in the Citadel complex. South of the river, the Americans occupied a complex that housed a local U.S. headquarters. PAVN troops moved against this outpost. There, about 200 U.S. soldiers and a few Australian troops held off the North Vietnamese forces.

As dawn came, the U.S. and South Vietnamese forces faced a distressing sight: The flag of North Vietnam flew from the flagpole above the Citadel. The effort to take down the flag would prove the longest and most difficult part of the fight to defeat the Tet Offensive.

Counterattack

The American and South Vietnamese troops responded to the Tet attacks very quickly. In some places, the defenders beat back the attackers and secured the areas right away. In others, such as around the Tan Son Nhut and Bien Hoa airbases, helicopters and armored carriers brought troops to the area that night.

While major combat ended quickly in several cities, it took some time for peace to be fully restored thereafter. Mortars exploded and gunfire broke out from time to time across the country for many days.

Viet Cong fighters had also holed up in residential areas in several cities. Some of them were so well hidden that it took many days to root them out.

The fight to retake Quang Tri, which was first attacked on the morning of January 31, 1968, showed the benefit of American mobility. U.S. armored cavalry forces were brought in to help the ARVN soldiers in Quang Tri, which was near North Vietnam. Helicopters landed troops at two sites to the east of the North Vietnamese army forces on the edge of the city. By landing there, they could trap the North Vietnamese soldiers between them and the ARVN troops to the west.

Once pushed out of the cities, Viet Cong combatants sometimes took refuge in outlying villages. American firepower was then directed at village bases to find the Viet Cong who had fled.

61

An American tank crew watched as a military bulldozer worked to clear away the rubble left behind by Tet fighting. Many cities in South Vietnam suffered major damage in the attack and counterattack.

At the same time, helicopters blasted the PAVN positions with rockets. Within a day, the PAVN resistance had weakened, and the soldiers began to withdraw. Helicopters pursued them as they left the battleground, adding to the already heavy North Vietnamese casualties.

In Quang Tri, as in other cities, success raised new problems. Retreating PAVN fighters tried to escape by joining the stream of civilian refugees moving away from the fighting. Across the South, U.S. military police and South Vietnamese soldiers set up checkpoints on the roads leading away from the fighting. They had to make sure that enemy fighters did not sneak away among the civilians.

SAIGON EXECUTION

City fighting produced one of the most dramatic images of the war. On February 1, a suspected Viet Cong officer was captured in Saigon. General Nguyen Ngoc Loan, chief of South Vietnam's police, pointed his pistol at the man's head at point blank range and executed him on the spot. The shooting was captured by a news photographer and a television camera crew. The images helped reinforce growing discomfort among many Americans with the way the war was going.

The fight to clear the PAVN out of Kontum, in the highlands of central Vietnam, took nearly two weeks. ARVN troops held key positions outside the city, while U.S. forces worked to drive North Vietnamese soldiers out of the city. That task required difficult house-to-house combat, but by February 4, less than a week after the attack, the city was clear.

The North Vietnamese troops then settled into the outlying towns around Kontum. After being pushed out of their hiding places, they took positions in nearby hills. U.S. and ARVN troops finally drove the North Vietnamese out of the hills near Kontum on February 12, 1968.

63

The attacks and counterattacks of Tet took a horrible toll on Vietnam's cities. U.S. and ARVN forces were forced to use massive firepower to blast the buildings that held Viet Cong and PAVN fighters. The result was major devastation in many areas.

One of the cities most damaged in the Tet attacks was Hué. Journalist Michael Herr described the devastation he saw after reaching the city a few days into the fighting:

> *Many of the houses had completely collapsed, and not one had been left without pitting from shell fragments. Hundreds of refugees held to the side of the road as we passed, many of them wounded.*

Within days of the attack by the People's Army of North Vietnam (PAVN), about 1,000 U.S. Marines and some tanks were sent to join the Americans at an outpost south of the Perfume River. Meanwhile, General Ngo Quang Truong gathered all his troops from the Army of the Republic of South Vietnam (ARVN) 1st Division north of the Citadel. Over time, both sides threw more troops into the battle. Several thousand more PAVN troops joined the forces that had captured the Citadel. They slipped in at nighttime, bringing supplies with them.

At first, the U.S. and ARVN forces divided the city. The Americans focused on the area south of the river. ARVN troops concentrated on winning back the Citadel.

On February 2, 1968, the counterattack began. The fighting was fierce, and progress was very slow. It took U.S. Marines six days to move four blocks from their starting position at the local Marine headquarters. In the process, 150 Marines were either killed or wounded. Used to fighting in the jungles, the Marines now had to adjust to city fighting. The combat was house to house, and the U.S. Marines worked in teams.

Civilians from the northern part of Hué fled across the Perfume River, hoping to find safety in the southern area of the city.

65

Four soldiers covered the exits, and two rushed the main door with grenades, while others gave them covering gunfire. The Marines tossed the grenades inside, hoping to flush out the enemy. If no one came out, they ran in with guns blazing. Once that house was secured, they moved to the next.

Sometimes the Marines used tanks or artillery to blast a house to pieces. A commander explained the reasoning:

CIVILIAN FEAR

Nguyen Qui Duc was a child living with his parents in Hué during the attack. He later remembered what it was like:

When the soldiers came into the house my mother screamed. We were completely terrified. They'd been described to us as atrocious, horrific people.

Later Duc and his mother watched the communist troops take his father away. He was held in the North for 12 years before he was finally released.

If you can save a Marine by destroying a house to get to [the enemy], then I say destroy the house.

It took until February 10 for the Marines to finally secure the southern part of the city. Even then, they continued to be attacked by PAVN mortar fire from across the river.

As the fighting raged on, helicopters brought supplies into the city and carried casualties out. The U.S. Navy had a loading area on the south shore of the Perfume River that they used to move equipment and wounded soldiers.

Meanwhile, U.S. Army troops had dropped in by parachute northwest of the city. Their job was to clear out the PAVN troops blocking Highway 1. They met stiff resistance, and 4,000 more Americans were sent to the area.

A team of U.S. Marines moved down a street in Hué, preparing to check each home for enemy fighters.

67

U.S. Marines returned fire as they moved across a bridge in Hué. Radio operators called in air strikes against the fighters threatening them.

ARVN troops had made some progress north of the Citadel but then stalled. They faced fierce resistance from an enemy that received fresh troops and supplies each night. By February 10, the ARVN troops held less than half of the Citadel. General Truong reluctantly asked for U.S. help.

On February 11, U.S. Marines crossed the river to join in the fight against the PAVN troops holding the Citadel. Despite heavy gunfire, they managed to complete the crossing. Two days later, they began the assault. The fight to capture the Citadel would last nearly two more weeks. As awful as the fight in the southern part of the city had been, this was worse. Casualties piled up. Almost half of all the Marines who fought in Hué were killed or wounded.

BURDENS OF WAR

Along with life-threatening conditions, the ARVN soldiers fighting in Hué faced additional burdens. Many had families living in the city and had no idea what had happened to them once the battle began. Their concern no doubt went beyond the usual worry that soldiers have for family members in war-torn areas, because they were in actual combat in the same areas their families were in. The ARVN soldiers also feared that enemy troops might punish their loved ones for supporting the South Vietnamese government. In addition, some ARVN fighters who were from Hué had to blow up their own homes to kill enemy soldiers hiding inside them.

But the Marines kept fighting. The government of South Vietnam had given them permission to bomb positions in the Citadel. The old imperial palace, though, was off limits. When the weather cleared, which was not often, planes swooped low and dropped napalm bombs, which started raging fires. The heavy shelling and firebombs were needed to drive out the PAVN troops. Journalist Michael Herr, who witnessed the bombing, wrote:

The [PAVN] had dug themselves so deeply into the wall that airstrikes had to open it meter by meter.

69

All the shelling could not clear the area of enemy soldiers, though. The Marines had to do that, once again advancing house by house. The layout of the Citadel made the job tougher. Houses were low and crowded together. Many streets were too narrow for tanks to travel along them. Thick trees and bushes grew all over the area, making it hard to see farther than 25 yards (23 m). The high walls that surrounded the complex offered perfect places for PAVN soldiers to hide. They could pepper advancing troops with machine gunfire from above.

People from the city of Hué searched through the rubble that used to be their homes, looking for any possessions they could reclaim.

The Americans took heavy casualties, and the PAVN troops did, too. By February 16, the PAVN commander grew desperate. He radioed his superiors for permission to withdraw but he was told to stay and fight.

On February 20, some Marines moved at night to seize a forward position. That helped the rest of the force move forward. By the next day, the Marines had finally taken hold of the northeast corner of the Citadel. It had taken them a week.

On February 22, the Marines moved closer to the imperial palace. Two days later, they were prepared to take the palace itself but new orders arrived: ARVN troops would take that last outpost.

The Black Panther Company of the ARVN was sent to recapture the imperial palace. Retaking the palace would be a reward for their bravery and skill in protecting the airport in Hué from enemy troops. They raced across the open field leading to the palace and ran inside but met no gunfire; the enemy was gone. The last troops had pulled out the previous night. The ARVN soldiers took down the flag of North Vietnam and raised the South Vietnamese flag.

The battle for Hué was finally over. After nearly four weeks of fighting, more than half the city had been destroyed. The great majority of the people of the city—116,000 out of 140,000—became refugees. It had been a bitter and bloody fight. ◤

Khe Sanh and Tet II

Chapter 7

While U.S. Marines and South Vietnamese army troops tried to clear Hué, fighting continued in other cities as well. Saigon was not cleared until March 7, 1968, and the Marine base in Khe Sanh was under shelling by the North Vietnamese into April.

By day, American pilots risked flying supplies into the base in Khe Sanh near the border of North and South Vietnam. They landed, unloaded, and took off as quickly as possible—sometimes in less than five minutes—to avoid the attacks of the People's Army of North Vietnam (PAVN). When the weather did not allow planes to land safely, helicopters brought supplies. However, neither could bring enough supplies to meet the Marines' needs for food, water, and ammunition.

The routine continued for weeks. PAVN troops shelled the U.S. soldiers with mortars and rockets. The Americans fired their own artillery and called in planes that bombed the PAVN positions. The Marines at Khe Sanh grew worried in early February when a nearby base was overrun. Each night they expected they would meet the same fate.

LANG VEI OVERRUN

On the night of February 7, 1968, PAVN troops attacked Lang Vei, a small outpost about 5 miles (8 km) west of Khe Sanh. U.S. and South Vietnamese soldiers held the camp. Suddenly, North Vietnamese troops and tanks hit the camp from three different directions. The soldiers in Lang Vei had little chance for survival. Nearly half were killed.

Within weeks, though, the PAVN attacks slowed. By early April 1968, the North Vietnamese broke off the attack and withdrew from the area. Marines went out cautiously to patrol the hills, ready to meet the enemy at any turn. But the trenches and camps were empty. The battle for Khe Sanh was over.

Marines manning a machine gun prepared for an attack on their position at Khe Sanh. Soldiers dug deep trenches to protect themselves from incoming gunfire.

Fighting in the South continued after Tet. It often resulted in the destruction of villages.

74

South Vietnam remained quiet only for a short time. In May, communist troops launched what historians refer to as Tet II. This was a new round of attacks on multiple sites across the country.

Many were simple mortar and rocket attacks that lasted a few nights and had little significance. Some of the combat was substantial, though.

About 8,000 PAVN troops moved across the border into Quang Tri province in northern South Vietnam to attack 5,000 American and ARVN troops at Dong Ha. That fight lasted three days before the PAVN retreated back north.

A special forces camp at Kham Duc, in northern South Vietnam, was also attacked by communist troops. The base was surrounded, and 1,800 U.S. and South Vietnamese soldiers and civilians there were trapped until air strikes pushed back the attackers. The camp was then evacuated.

Heavy fighting took place in Saigon, starting on May 5, 1968, and again on May 25. Thousands of PAVN troops moved into the city, threatening airports, bridges, and other key sites. U.S. and ARVN troops needed about two weeks to dislodge each attack. They had to use intense firepower, including rockets and napalm. The result was widespread destruction. In one section of the city, 8,000 homes were destroyed in five days. ◣

The Impact of the Tet Offensive

The cost of the Tet Offensive and the allied counterattack was high. Many cities in South Vietnam suffered extensive damage. About half of the city of Pleiku was destroyed, and nearly a quarter of Ban Me Thuot and Da Lat were turned into rubble as well.

Civilians suffered, too. Exact numbers are not clear, but approximately 15,000 civilians are thought to have been killed with another 20,000 wounded as a result of the fighting. It is estimated that half a million people were driven from their homes and became refugees.

Approximately 1,100 U.S. soldiers were killed, and nearly 3,000 were wounded. South Vietnamese troops were also hit hard with 2,300 ARVN soldiers reported dead, and a few thousand more wounded.

For the communists, the Tet Offensive had mixed results. The exact number of North Vietnamese and Viet Cong killed and wounded is unknown. American estimates put the number killed at 40,000 to 50,000, but those estimates are probably high.

Still, it is clear that Viet Cong losses, in particular, were heavy. But according to some reports, the losses did not cripple the communists. Only a small part of the North Vietnamese army took part in the Tet Offensive. In the spring of 1968, U.S. officials believed that as many as 40,000 PAVN troops had already moved south to keep pressure on U.S. and South Vietnamese troops. As a result, the Viet Cong were able to rebound from their losses. By 1971, the Viet Cong were once again regaining power in the countryside.

In military terms, Tet looked like a defeat for the communists. They had heavy losses and had not kept control of any buildings, facilities, or cities. Nor did the attacks produce a general uprising across South Vietnam, as the communists had hoped would occur.

A VIET CONG VIEW OF TET

The Viet Cong suffered badly in Tet. Trinh Duc was a National Liberation Front leader in Long Khanh province, northeast of Saigon. He later recalled the difficult situation:

The Tet Offensive brought on the worst time of the war. First of all, casualties everywhere were very, very high, and the spirit of the soldiers dropped to a low point. Secondly, afterwards the enemy changed over to what we called the "two-pincer strategy." They began to send out guerrilla forces to ambush us in the jungle. After a while there was nowhere to turn.

The Tet Offensive did have some political success for the Viet Cong. General Westmoreland admitted this in a report back to Washington, D.C.:

> We must accept the fact that the enemy has dealt the [government of South Vietnam] a severe blow. He has brought the war to the towns and cities and has inflicted damage and casualties on the population. Distribution of the necessities has been interrupted ... and the economy has been disrupted. The people have felt directly the impact of the war.

Attacks on the cities—and the ferocity of the allied counterattacks—stirred unrest across the South. While the attackers were driven off, the effort to dislodge them left ruined cities and displaced people in its wake. That undermined

After Tet, the fighting did not let up. U.S. pilots participated in bombing missions aimed at communist troops in northern South Vietnam. The bombings came under more criticism from people in the United States toward the end of the war.

support for the Americans and the government of South Vietnam. One refugee said:

> *The Viet Cong offensive is like the tide lapping at a beach. It comes and it goes. But each time, a little bit of the government's authority is swept away.*

After the fighting, South Vietnam's government tried to solve some of its problems. President Nguyen Van Thieu, South Vietnam's president since 1967, extended his country's draft to make the army larger. He removed from command some of the generals who had performed poorly during Tet. He also took steps to prevent officers from becoming wealthy through corruption. In the end, though, such problems continued to plague South Vietnam throughout the remainder of the war.

Tet's most profound political effects came in the United States. The widespread attacks shook the confidence of many officials in Washington, D.C.

In late February 1968, General Westmoreland asked Washington for more than 200,000 additional troops. The request shocked many Johnson advisers since the general, only the previous fall, had been so optimistic.

President Johnson ordered Clark Clifford, who would soon become secretary of defense, to consider the request. Clifford reported back that the government should agree to send Westmoreland only 20,000 troops and keep an eye on the situation before taking any further action.

Polls showed that public approval of the war was on a downward slide. In the midst of that decline, television reporter Walter Cronkite traveled to Vietnam to study the war effort. Cronkite was just

DECLINING SUPPORT

In 1965, more than 60 percent of Americans told public opinion surveys that sending troops to Vietnam was not a mistake. Over the next three years, that support steadily fell. By late 1967, more people thought the war was a mistake than not. More revealing was the American view of President Johnson. In 1965, about 60 percent of the people approved of how he handled the war. Just before the Tet Offensive, that approval had fallen to less than 40 percent. In March 1968, the president's approval rating would plummet to 26 percent. However, some historians think these figures might be misleading. Many Americans never made up their minds about whether they supported the U.S. war effort.

one of many journalists who now viewed the war as impossible to win. On his return, Cronkite gave a gloomy report:

> *To say we are closer to victory today is to believe ... optimists who have been wrong in the past. To suggest we are on the edge of defeat is to yield to unreasonable pessimists. To say we are mired in stalemate seems the only realistic ... conclusion.*

While the fighting raged in South Vietnam, bombing of North Vietnam continued. The North Vietnamese used anti-aircraft guns to try to down U.S. bombers.

Antiwar rallies were staged more frequently in the months after the Tet Offensive.

Meanwhile, President Johnson faced another challenge. He was running for reelection. The first test was in the state of New Hampshire, where his Democratic party held a primary. In this kind of

82

HELL NO
WE WON'T
GO!! ☮

We Need

election, voters choose who they want to be the political party's nominee for president.

Senator Eugene McCarthy of Minnesota ran a campaign strongly against the war. President Johnson won the March 12 primary as expected. However, he only captured 49 percent of the vote. McCarthy won 42 percent, a very strong showing for a man who had not been well-known before. The vote showed that Johnson was in political trouble because of the war.

Within days, New York Senator Robert Kennedy announced that he would also try to win the Democratic nomination for president. He, too, would run against the war. Johnson knew that Kennedy would make a tough opponent.

The Tet Offensive and Westmoreland's request for huge numbers of extra troops had shaken President Johnson. In late March, he held a meeting with several highly respected men who had served in past governments. These advisers included former Secretary of State Dean Acheson; former foreign policy advisers George Ball and McGeorge Bundy; Henry Cabot Lodge, who had twice been U.S. ambassador to South Vietnam; and generals Omar Bradley and Matthew Ridgway.

Almost all of them told Johnson that the war could not be won as it was now being fought. Several urged him to stop the bombing of North Vietnam. Within days, Johnson agreed to a halt to the bombing.

President Johnson spoke on television on March 31, 1968, and announced a halt to the bombing in Vietnam in an effort to persuade communist leaders to begin peace talks. In that speech, Johnson also said he was giving up his run for the presidency.

On March 31, Johnson made his decision public. In a television address, he said that the bombing would stop as a gesture to persuade North Vietnam to begin peace talks to end the war. In a stunning closing, Johnson said that he would not run for reelection. Though the U.S. military might have won the overall battle of the Tet Offensive, the U.S. president had suffered a political defeat.

Peace talks began later in 1968 but dragged on for years. U.S. casualties continued to rise. President Richard Nixon, elected in 1968 and again in 1972, launched a policy of gradually reducing the number of U.S. troops in Vietnam. Troop levels started to fall in 1969. In 1973, the United States, South Vietnam, North Vietnam, and the National Liberation Front signed a peace treaty. All parties agreed to stop fighting and return prisoners of war they held. American forces would leave South Vietnam. Though North Vietnam's troops could stay in the South, its leaders pledged to stop fighting. The last U.S. combat troops left in March.

Still, the fighting continued. In 1975, North Vietnamese forces unleashed a massive offensive into the South. The army of South Vietnam collapsed, and the government surrendered on April 30, 1975. Vietnam was, finally, a united country.

The Vietnam War had been a costly conflict in lives and public funds for North Vietnam, the Viet Cong, South Vietnam, and the United States. Much of Vietnam lay in ruins after years of bombing and fighting. Thousands fled South Vietnam, fearing that communist rule would produce arrests and executions, as it had in Hué. Those who could not afford to leave stayed, hoping that after decades of conflict they could get on with their lives.

The war left American society badly divided. Those who had opposed the war felt that the South's collapse had proved that they were right. Military leaders were demoralized, feeling that they had not been supported by the country as a whole. Many pointed to the Tet Offensive as the key turning point in the war. Antiwar protesters said it showed that the North could not have been defeated. Those who had supported the war argued that it proved that the military could have won but that the country's leaders had let the soldiers down. That debate continues today. ◣

Timeline

September 2, 1945

Ho Chi Minh declares independence of Vietnam

November–December 1946

War between Vietnam and France begins

May 7, 1954

French surrender to Viet Minh at Dien Bien Phu

July 1954

Geneva Accords end war between France and Vietnam and set forth temporary division of the country

July 16, 1955

Ngo Dinh Diem, with U.S. support, refuses to take part in reunification elections

December 20, 1960

Viet Cong formed to overthrow the government of South Vietnam

November 1963

Ngo Dinh Diem is assassinated in military takeover in South Vietnam

November 22, 1963

Lyndon Johnson sworn in as U.S. president after President John F. Kennedy is assassinated

August 2, 1964

North Vietnamese boats attack U.S. destroyer in the Gulf of Tonkin

August 7, 1964

U.S. Congress passes Gulf of Tonkin Resolution giving President Johnson broad power to fight in Vietnam

March 2, 1965

Operation Rolling Thunder—extreme bombing of North Vietnam—begins

October 1965

U.S. forces defeat North Vietnamese troops in extended battle at Plei Me

November 1965

U.S. forces defeat North Vietnamese troops in Ia Drang valley

December 31, 1965

U.S. troop strength in South Vietnam now 200,000

July 7, 1967

Politburo of North Vietnam approves military and general uprising

November 3, 1967

North Vietnamese troops attack Dak To

December 31, 1967

 U.S. troop strength in South Vietnam nearly 500,000

January 21, 1968

Fighting begins at Khe Sanh

January 30, 1968

First Tet attacks at Nha Trang and other cities in northern South Vietnam

January 31, 1968

 Main Tet attacks, including Saigon, Hué, and many other targets; U.S. Embassy attacked in Saigon

February 2, 1968

Counterattack begins in Hué

February 8, 1968

Lang Vei overrun by North Vietnamese troops

February 10, 1968

U.S. Marines finish clearing enemy troops out of southern Hué

February 12, 1968

Fighting in Kontum declared over

February 25, 1968

Fighting in Hué ends

February 27, 1968

Walter Cronkite broadcast includes gloomy evaluation of the war

March 7, 1968

Fighting in Saigon declared over

March 12, 1968

President Johnson narrowly defeats Senator Eugene McCarthy in the New Hampshire Democratic primary

March 16, 1968

Senator Robert Kennedy declares he will run against Johnson for the Democratic nomination for president

March 31, 1968

 Johnson announces halt to bombing and decision to not seek reelection

April 8, 1968

Battle at Khe Sanh over after North Vietnamese withdraw

Timeline

May 5, 1968

Fighting in Saigon during Tet II

May 13, 1968

First meeting of Paris peace talks

May 25, 1968

Renewed fighting in Saigon

July 3, 1968

Westmoreland replaced as overall U.S. commander in Vietnam

July 5, 1968

Marine base at Khe Sanh abandoned

November 5, 1968

Richard Nixon elected president of the United States

December 31, 1968

U.S. troop strength in Vietnam at about 540,000

June 8, 1969

Nixon announces first American troop withdrawals from Vietnam

September 3, 1969

Ho Chi Minh dies

December 31, 1970

U.S. troop strength in Vietnam now about 280,000

January 27, 1973

Cease-fire agreement signed in Paris by all parties

March 29, 1973

Last U.S. troops leave South Vietnam

January 1975

North Vietnam unleashes last offensive

April 30, 1975

South Vietnam surrenders after capture of Saigon

ON THE WEB

For more information on *The Tet Offensive,* use FactHound.

1 Go to *www.facthound.com*

2 Type in a search word related to this book or this book ID: 0756516234

3 Click on the *Fetch It* button. FactHound will find Web sites related to this book.

HISTORIC SITES

Vietnam Veterans Memorial
900 Ohio Drive S.W.
Washington, DC 20024
202/426-6841

"The Wall" lists and pays tribute to every member of the U.S. armed forces killed in the Vietnam War.

Vietnam War Museum
954 W. Carmen Ave.
Chicago, IL 60640
773/728-6111

Exhibits, documents, and artwork revealing the history of the war

LOOK FOR ALL THE BOOKS IN THIS SERIES

The Cuban Missile Crisis:
To the Brink of War
ISBN 0-7565-1624-2

Hiroshima and Nagasaki:
Fire from the Sky
ISBN 0-7565-1621-8

The Korean War:
America's Forgotten War
ISBN 0-7565-1625-0

Pearl Harbor:
Day of Infamy
ISBN 0-7565-1622-6

September 11:
Attack on America
ISBN 0-7565-1620-X

The Tet Offensive:
Turning Point of the Vietnam War
ISBN 0-7565-1623-4

Glossary

armored personnel carrier

a heavily armored vehicle used to carry troops

artillery

powerful weapons that fire rockets or shells

ARVN

the Army of the Republic of South Vietnam; the regular troops of South Vietnam's army

casualties

the people killed, wounded, or missing in a battle or in a war

communist

country or person practicing communism, a political system in which there is no private property and everything is owned and shared in common

delta

the area of rich farmland formed by the mouth of a river

embassy

a building that serves as official headquarters of the ambassador sent to represent one country in another nation

infantry

the branch of an army made up of units trained to fight on foot

M-16

the standard rifle used by U.S. soldiers during the Vietnam War

mortar

a small piece of artillery used by individual soldiers to shoot explosive shells

military police (MP)

a member of the military who guards buildings and polices other people serving in the armed forces

mine

small explosive device buried in the ground that is set off when a person steps on it or a vehicle moves over it

napalm

a highly flammable chemical used in flame throwers and bombs

National Liberation Front (NLF)

a political organization that aimed to overthrow the government of South Vietnam

PAVN

the People's Army of North Vietnam; the regular troops of North Vietnam

Viet Cong

South Vietnamese rebels who tried to overthrow the government of South Vietnam and who were aided by the government of North Vietnam

Source Notes

Chapter 1

Page 10, sidebar: David Chanoff and Doan Van Toai. *Portrait of the Enemy.* New York: Random House, 1986, pp. 160–161.

Page 10, line 20: "VC Assault on the U.S. Embassy." 23 Nov. 2005 <http://historynet.com/vn/blvcassaultonembassy>

Page 13, line 8: Don Oberdorfer. *Tet! The Turning Point in the Vietnam War.* Baltimore, Md.: Johns Hopkins University Press, 2001, p. 23.

Page 17, line 13: Ibid., p. 34.

Chapter 2

Page 20, line 4: Stanley Karnow. *Vietnam: A History.* New York: Viking Press, 1983, p. 135.

Chapter 3

Page 29, line 13: Marc Jason Gilbert and William Head, eds. *The Tet Offensive.* Westport, Conn.: Praeger, 1996, p. 82.

Page 32, line 19: Christian G. Appy. *Patriots: The Vietnam War Remembered from All Sides.* New York: Penguin Books, 2003, pp. 302–303.

Page 34, line 13: *The Tet Offensive,* p. 146.

Page 35, line 14: *Tet! The Turning Point in the Vietnam War,* p. 121.

Page 39, line 4: *Vietnam: A History,* p. 540.

Chapter 4

Page 41, line 3: *Tet! The Turning Point in the Vietnam War,* pp. 67–68.

Page 42, line 2: Clark Dougan, Stephen Weiss, and editors. *Nineteen Sixty-Eight.* Boston: Boston Publishing Company, 1984, p. 12.

SOURCE NOTES

Chapter 5

Page 48, line 7: *Tet! The Turning Point in the Vietnam War,* pp. 131–132.

Page 50, sidebar: Wallace Terry. *Bloods: An Oral History of the Vietnam War by Black Veterans.* New York: Random House, 1984, p. 118.

Page 50, line 28: John J. Tolson. *Airmobility 1961–1971.* Washington, D.C.: U.S. Government Printing Office, 1973, p. 157.

Chapter 6

Page 64, line 11: Michael Herr. *Reporting Vietnam: American Journalism 1959–1975.* New York: Library of America, 2000, pp. 314–315.

Page 66, sidebar: *Patriots: The Vietnam War Remembered from All Sides,* pp. 295–296.

Page 66, line 19: *Nineteen Sixty-Eight,* p. 291.

Page 69, line 29: *Reporting Vietnam: American Journalism 1959–1975,* p. 320.

Chapter 8

Page 77, sidebar: *Portrait of the Enemy,* p. 107.

Page 78, line 4: Robert J. McMahon, ed. *Major Problems in the History of the Vietnam War.* Boston: Houghton Mifflin, 2003, p. 337.

Page 79, line 3: *Nineteen Sixty-Eight,* p. 147.

Page 81, line 4: *Major Problems in the History of the Vietnam War,* p. 351.

SELECT BIBLIOGRAPHY

Appy, Christian G. *Patriots: The Vietnam War Remembered from All Sides.*
New York: Penguin Books, 2003.

Arnold, James R. *Tet Offensive 1968: Turning Point in Vietnam.* Oxford,
England: Osprey Publishing, 1990.

Chanoff, David, and Doan Van Toai. *Portrait of the Enemy.* New York:
Random House, 1986.

Dougan, Clark, and Stephen Weiss, and editors. *Nineteen Sixty-Eight.*
Boston: Boston Publishing Company, 1983.

Ebert, James R. *A Life in a Year: The American Infantryman in Vietnam.*
New York: Ballantine Books, 1993.

Gilbert, Marc Jason, and William Head, eds. *The Tet Offensive.*
Westport, Conn.: Praeger, 1996.

Karnow, Stanley. *Vietnam: A History.* New York: Viking Press, 1983.

McMahon, Robert J., ed. *Major Problems in the History of the Vietnam War.*
Boston: Houghton Mifflin, 2003.

Nolan, Keith William. *Battle for Hue: Tet 1968.* Novato, Calif.: Novato
Press, 1996.

Oberdorfer, Don. *Tet! The Turning Point in the Vietnam War.*
Baltimore, Md.: Johns Hopkins University Press, 2001.

Terry, Wallace. *Bloods: An Oral History of the Vietnam War by Black Veterans.*
New York: Random House, 1984.

FURTHER READING

Canwell, Diane, and Jon Sutherland. *African Americans in the
Vietnam War.* New York: World Almanac Library, 2004.

Isserman, Maurice. *Vietnam War.* New York: Facts on File, 2004.

Willoughby, Douglas. *The Vietnam War.* Chicago: Heinemann
Library, 2001.

Index

ABOUT THE AUTHOR

Dale Anderson studied history and literature at Harvard College. He has worked in publishing ever since. He now lives with his wife and two sons in Newtown, Pennsylvania, where he writes and edits textbooks and library books. He has written several books for young adults, including a multivolume series on the Civil War, *The Cold War Years,* and *America into a New Millennium.*

IMAGE CREDITS